First Lesso
Voice

by Michaela Anne Neller

1 2 3 4 5 6 7 8 9 0

Visit us on the Web at www.melbay.com — E-mail us at email@melbay.com

Table of Contents

Introduction:
Basic Techniques of Singing

Just like a guitar, saxophone, piano, clarinet or flute, the voice is an instrument that requires training and education if one wishes to improve upon their natural ability. Understanding the parts of the voice, how it functions, and routinely practicing will help your voice gain flexibility, agility, a wider range, and ultimately more control to consistently sing what you hear in your head.

Unlike those other instruments, the voice is a part of your anatomy and is carried with you at all times. This means the voice requires unique care and awareness that other instruments do not. In this book you will learn about the anatomy of your voice and breathing system, safe and healthy technique for singing as well as breathing and how to properly care for your voice within your lifestyle.

You will also learn the basics of the piano and music theory. Having this foundational knowledge will enable you to create and conduct exercises on your own as well as confidently learn new songs from lead sheets. Reading music notation is an important skill to have no matter what instrument you play and opens you up to many more exciting musical experiences.

The book includes a number of exercises as well as songs for you to practice singing.

Fundamentals of Music

Music is written on a staff which consists of five lines and four spaces.

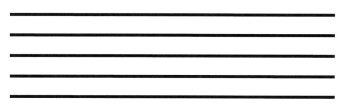

What letter a note correlates to is determined by where it sits within the lines and spaces of the staff.

Treble Clef

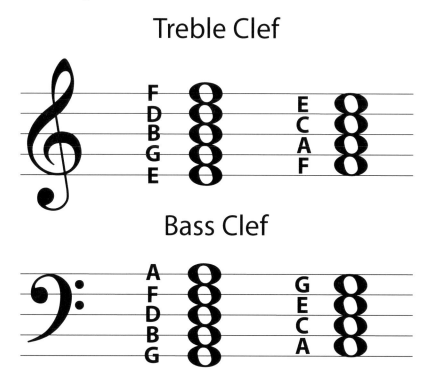

Bass Clef

A few easy ways to remember the letter names:

➢ Treble clef lines can be remembered by the sentence **E**very **G**ood **B**oy **D**oes **F**ine.

➢ Treble clef Spaces spell out **FACE**

➢ Bass clef lines can be remembered by the sentence **G**ood **B**oys **D**o **F**ine **A**lways

➢ Bass clef spaces can be remembered by the sentence **A**ll **C**ows **E**at **G**rass

The clefs, as referred to on the previous page, determine the pitch range of the notes written on that staff.

The treble clef indicates the upper range.

The bass clef indicates the lower range.

They correlate to the piano as follows:

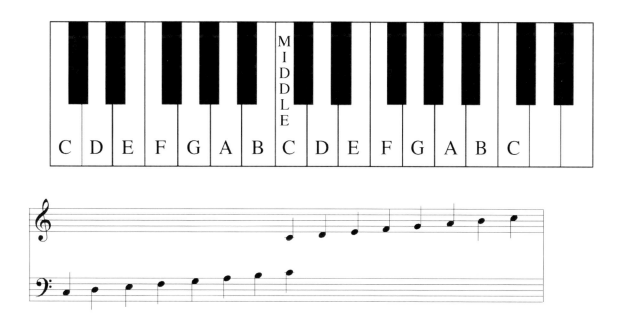

The staff is then divided into measures with vertical lines called bars. A double bar indicates the end of a section or the end of the song.

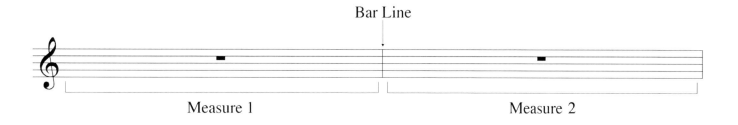

5

Notes

A note indicates which pitch to sing depending on where it lies within the staff. The different kinds of notes represent different lengths of time the pitch should be held.

Types of Notes:

Whole note = receives four beats or counts

Half note = receives two beats or counts

Quarter note = receives one beat or count

Eighth note = receives one-half beat or count

Rests

A rest is an interval of silence within the music. Each different rest indicates a different duration of time the silence should be held.

Whole rest = four beats or counts of silence

Half rest = two beats or counts of silence

Quarter rest = one beat or count of silence

Eighth rest = one-half beat or count of silence

Time Signatures

Some common time signatures that will be used in this book are:

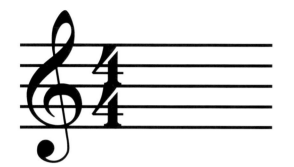

4/4 is the most common time signature. It can also be notated with a C literally meaning "common time".

Number of beats per measure > **2** < Beats per measure

The type of note receiving one beat > **4** < The quarter note receives one beat

PIANO

Becoming familiar with the notes of the piano is extremely helpful for any singer. This will enable you to play your own exercises as well as learn songs from their written form.

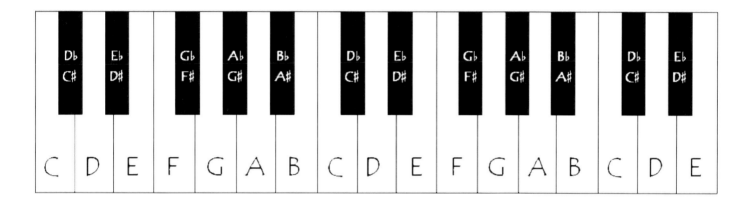

Chords, Triads, scales and arpeggios

A few common terms that will be used within the vocal exercises.

➢ A **chord** is a set of harmonically related notes played simultaneously. A **triad** is a type of chord consisting of only three notes.

➢ A **scale** is a series of different pitches played in succession rather than simultaneously, according to a specific scheme.

➢ An **arpeggio** is the sounding of the notes in a chord played in succession rather than simultaneously.

The Physical Act of Singing

Understanding the physical anatomy of your voice and body is vital to taking proper care of your voice as well as learning to use it in a healthy, non-harmful manner.

In the most simple of terms, the voice is made up of your **larynx** which sits at the top of your wind pipe and holds your **vocal cords**. The vocal cords are two folds made up of a thin strip of cartilage. The folds open and close against the escaping air to create sound. As the sound moves up and out through the back of your mouth it will pass beneath the raised **soft palate**.

The soft palate is the soft tissue that is at the back end of the roof of your mouth. To find where your soft palate is, run your tongue along the roof of your mouth, beginning behind your upper teeth. When the texture changes from hard to soft, you have reached the soft palate. This soft tissue can raise and lower. When singing, the soft palate should always be raised in order to make room for the flow of sound. As an exercise, try a yawn. You'll feel your soft palate rise. If it continues to rise, you will progress into a yawn. That moment right before the yawn is how it should feel when singing.

The shape of your mouth strongly determines the sound that is produced. A relaxed jaw with an open mouth focusing the sound up through the roof of your mouth and out is ideal. The tongue should be relaxed and resting behind your lower teeth. If the tongue rises other than to pronounce consonants it can block the flow of sound.

Exercise 1

The siren is a great exercise to really feel the natural and relaxed flow of sound through an open mouth and throat as well as the lifting of the soft palate. Start on an open vowel, either U or A and gently slide up chromatically. Continue to the highest note you can comfortably reach and begin to gently slide back down.

To notate the siren I will use a **slur**. A **slur** is a symbol that indicates that the notes within the slur should be played without separation.

Initial Checklist

Each time you sing you should run through a quick mental check list to note a healthy relaxed positioning of your mouth and jaw.

➤ Jaw relaxed and level.
>   This is important. Do not tense your jaw or reach for notes with your chin and throat. Your chin should be level and in a relaxed manner at all times. You should not feel any pain or discomfort when singing.

➤ Soft palate raised.
>   Like the beginning of a yawn the soft palate should be raised to create an open and unblocked throughway for the sound.

➤ Tongue resting naturally behind back of lower teeth.
>   The tongue should only move to pronounce consonants and should otherwise be resting in the lower position as to clear the way for the travel of sound.

➤ Relaxed open mouth focusing flow of sound up and out.
>   A relaxed open mouth creates an optimal shape to create a resonant beautiful tone.

Guidelines to Vocal Health

Our voice is a body part and therefore is affected by our diet, exercise, sleep, habits and environment. As singers, we carry our instrument with us everywhere and use it on a daily basis. It is important to be sensitive to this and treat your voice with care. You want it to last a lifetime.

We all learn how to listen to our bodies and determine how different things will affect us. As you pay attention and continue to sing, you will also learn what affects the strength, quality and flexibility of your voice. With that in mind, here are some guidelines to follow for strong vocal health.

➢ **Hydration**. Drink lots of water. Staying well hydrated will lubricate your vocal cords and increase flexibility and strength.

➢ **Warmups**. Just like our muscles need to stretch and warm up before a run, vocal cords benefit from warming up before singing. The exercises provided in this book are great ways to start any vocal session. Be careful not to strain or push your vocal cords at any time. Be especially gentle at the start of a warmup.

➢ **Smoking**. Don't do it. Inhaling hot smoke damages the mucous membranes of your larynx as well as diminishes your lung capacity. If you want strong breath support and flexible vocal cords, stay away from smoking of any kind.

➢ **Sleep**. Be well rested. Just like the rest of your body, your voice functions at the highest level when it has adequate rest and therefore optimal strength. Take care of yourself.

➢ **Food**. As stated before, we all learn what and how different things affect our bodies. Eating a well-balanced healthy diet is ideal for a strong healthy voice. The general rule is that anything that causes excess mucous or dries out your vocal cords should be avoided. This includes dairy, sugar and caffeine. Be conscious of how these things affect you and remember moderation is always key.

Breathing

Understanding and practicing proper breathing technique leads to having adequate support to sustain notes and sing safely with strength and power.

Many of us misunderstand breathing and learn to breathe by expanding our chests because we associate breathing with our lungs rather than the diaphragm. Instead of expanding our lungs we should be expanding our abdomen to make room for the diaphragm to do it's job. The diaphragm is a dome-shaped muscle that divides the body in half just below the lungs. Its job is to lower and make room for the lungs to fill with our air. As it contracts, it flattens out and pushes your digestive system out of the way to make room for the lungs to increase in size, therefore filling with the most air they can hold.

As the diaphragm flattens, the rib cage expands. You will feel this most intensely through the lower rib cage and into your abdomen. As you inhale you should feel the expansion. As you exhale, you should deflate like a balloon.

Proper relaxed posture, with a straight back and relaxed chest and shoulders, is important to guarantee proper function of your diaphragm. Try some of the exercises below to practice breathing with this technique. Gently placing your hands around your abdomen, sides and back will help you feel the expansion and deflation.

Exercise 2A

Sustaining a note for as long as you can is as much about how much air you take in as it is about how much air you release at the start of your note. A nice strong intake of air is vital but if you blow it all out the moment you open your mouth, you won't be able to sustain a long note. Try these next exercises to practice breath control while releasing air throughout a phrase slowly and steadily.

Without singing a particular pitch, take a deep breath in and release slowly on the sound **Hisssssssssssssssssss,** like a snake. Your teeth should be close together which makes it easier to conserve your air. Do this multiple times attempting to improve upon the length of time you can hissss.

Exercise 2B

Engaging your stomach muscles is vital for strong breath support. You should feel your abdomen deflate when you exert air for a note or sound. If it is a staccato note, your muscles should deflate strongly and pull in quickly with each note. **Staccato** is a musical articulation that signifies a clear-cut playing or sounding of the note disconnected from the sounds before or after. Try it on this exercise below.

Strongly whisper, without singing a particular pitch, the first four beats staccato. The last beat hold out as long as you can.

Hee! Hee! Hee! Hee! Heeeeeeeeee

Now try all of the vowels

Hah! Hah! Hah! Hah! Haaaaaaaaaaahhhhhh
Heh! Heh! Heh! Heh! Heeeeeeeeeehhhhhh
Hoh! Hoh! Hoh! Hoh! Hoooooohhhh
Hoo! Hoo! Hoo! Hoo! Hooooooooooo

VOWELS

Throughout this book's exercises you will often encounter pure vowels. This refers to the open pronunciation of our vowels AEIOU.

A: Ah as in (Awe)some
E: Eh as in T(a)ble
I: Ee as in Tr(ee)
O: Oh as in L(o)w
U: Oo as in Oops

To focus on feeling the expansion of your abdomen, sides and back when breathing properly, try these exercises while lying on your back. When you breathe in you should feel everything expand and inflate. The resistance from the floor will cause you to slightly rise.

 Exercise 3   **Exercise 3 Instrumental**

Ma Me Mi Mo Mu

 **Exercise 4** **Exercise 4 Instrumental**

This next exercise is great to incorporate strong and engaged breathing with sounding pitches. You will use a hard H and sing staccato notes on a triad. You should feel your abdomen quickly deflate at each Ha.

For Exercises 5 and 6, start out singing with the consonant M attached to the vowels, but as you progress experiment with different consonants.

Try Fi Fe Fa Fo Fu or Li Le La Lo Lu and even advance to double consonants like Thi The Tha Tho Thu or Shi She Sha Sho Shu.

The idea is to get used to singing with consonants while preserving the resonance that is more easily reached with open vowels.

For all exercises, try them throughout your range on the piano moving up and down octaves. Don't limit yourself to only what is written here and heared on the audio.

 Exercise 5   **Exercise 5 Instrumental**

Mi Me Ma Mo Mu (Up in Thirds)

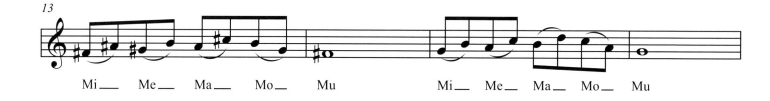

18

Mi ___ Me ___ Ma ___ Mo ___ Mu

Mi ___ Me ___ Ma ___ Mo ___ Mu

Mi ___ Me ___ Ma ___ Mu

Mi ___ Me ___ Ma ___ Mu

Mi ___ Me ___ Ma ___ Mu.

 **Exercise 6**   **Exercise 6 Instrumental**

Mi Me Ma Mo Mu (down in thirds)

Mi ___ Me ___ Ma ___ Mo ___ Mu

Mi ___ Me ___ Ma ___ Mo ___ Mu

Mi ___ Me ___ Ma ___ Mo ___ Mu

Mi ___ Me ___ Ma ___ Mo ___ Mu

Mi ___ Me ___ Ma ___ Mo ___ Mu

Mi ___ Me ___ Ma ___ Mo ___ Mu

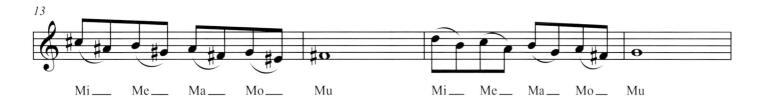

Mi ___ Me ___ Ma ___ Mo ___ Mu

Mi ___ Me ___ Ma ___ Mo ___ Mu

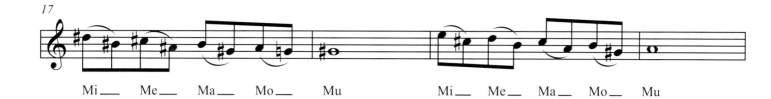

Mi___ Me___ Ma___ Mo___ Mu   Mi___ Me___ Ma___ Mo___ Mu

Mi___ Me___ Ma___ Mo___ Mu   Mi___ Me___ Ma___ Mo___ Mu.

Exercise 7

Let's now focus on some sustained thirds in the lower and upper registers. The example tracks have a different vowel for each section of this exercise. Go through and try every vowel for each exercise when you are practicing on your own.

 **Part A**    **Exercise 7 Part A Instrumental**

Sustained Ah Ah up a major third in lower register

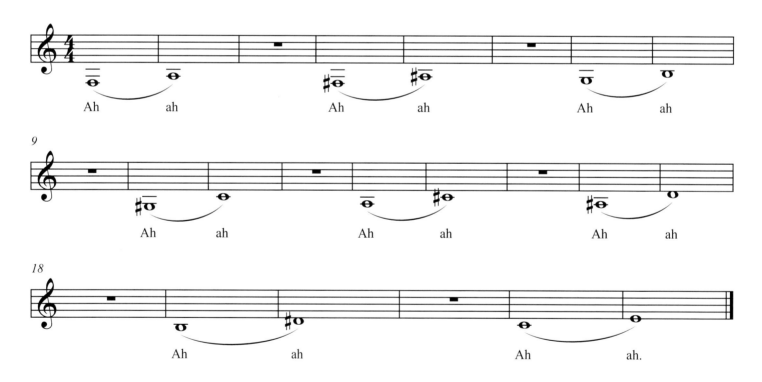

 **Part B**   **Exercise 7 Part B Instrumental**

Sustained Oo Oo up a major third in upper register

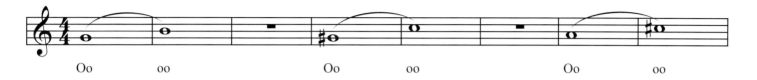

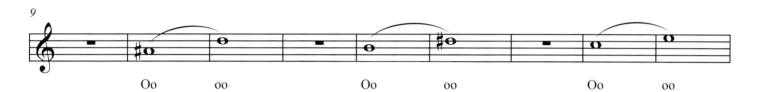

Now try the same exercise in Part C and D in both registers using a minor third instead.

Part C   **Exercise 7 Part C Instrumental**

 **Part D**

 Exercise 7 Part D Instrumental

Ee ee Ee Ee Ee ee

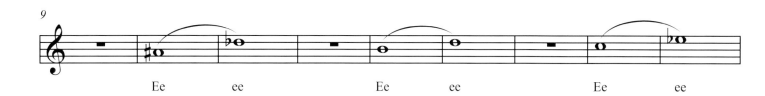

Ee ee Ee ee Ee ee

Ee ee Ee ee

This exercise sings the first 5 scale tones in a major scale. Sing on La.

La la   la la la la la la   la   la la la   la   la la la la la   la   la   la   la la la la la la   la

la la la la la la la la   la   la   la   la   la   la la la la   la   la   la   la   la la la la la   la

la la la   la   la la la la   la   la   la   la la la la la la   la   la la la   la la la la la la   la

la   la   la la   la la la la   la   la la la la la la la la   la   la   la   la   la   la la la la la   la

la la   la la la la la la   la   la   la   la   la   la la la la   la   la   la   la   la   la la la la la   la

la la la la la la la la la   la la la la la la la la la   la la la la la la la la la

la la la la la la la la la   la la la la la la la la la   la la la la la la la la la

la la la la la la la la la   la la la la la la la la la   la la la la la la la la la

la la la la la la la la la   la la la la la la la la la   la la la la la la la la la

la la la la la la la la la

Try this arpeggio exercise all the way through on each different vowel.
Feel free to expand the exercise to lower or higher ranges as well.

Ah ah ah ah ah ah ah   Ah ah ah ah ah ah ah   Ah ah ah ah ah ah ah
Eh eh eh eh eh eh eh   Eh eh eh eh eh eh eh   Eh eh eh eh eh eh eh
Ee ee ee ee ee ee ee   Eh ee ee ee ee ee ee   Ee ee ee ee ee ee ee
Oh oh oh oh oh oh oh   Oh oh oh oh oh oh oh   Oh oh oh oh oh oh oh
Oo oo oo oo oo oo oo   Oo oo oo oo oo oo oo   Oo oo oo oo oo oo oo

Ah ah ah ah ah aha ha   Ah ah ah ah ah ah ah   Ah ah ah ah ah ah ah   Ah ah ah ah ah ah ah
Eh eh eh eh eh eh eh   Eh eh eh eh eh eh eh   Eh eh eh eh eh eh eh   Eh eh eh eh eh eh eh
Ee ee ee ee ee ee ee   Ee ee ee ee ee ee ee   Ee ee ee ee ee ee ee   Ee ee ee ee ee ee ee
Oh oh oh oh oh oh oh   Oh oh oh oh oh oh oh   Oh oh oh oh oh oh oh   Oh oh oh oh oh oh oh
Oo oo oo oo oo oo oo   Oo oo oo oo oo oo oo   Oo oo oo oo oo oo oo   Oo oo oo oo oo oo oo

Ah ah ah ah ah ah ah   Ah ah ah ah ah ah ah   Ah ah ah ah ah ah ah   Ah ah ah ah ah ah ah
Eh eh eh eh eh eh eh   Eh eh eh eh eh eh eh   Eh eh eh eh eh eh eh   Eh eh eh eh eh eh eh
Ee ee ee ee ee ee ee   Ee ee ee ee ee ee ee   Ee ee ee ee ee ee ee   Ee ee ee ee ee ee ee
Oh oh oh oh oh oh oh   Oh oh oh oh oh oh oh   Oh oh oh oh oh oh oh   Oh oh oh oh oh oh oh
Oo oo oo oo oo oo oo   Oo oo oo oo oo oo oo   Oo oo oo oo oo oo oo   Oo oo oo oo oo oo oo

Ah ah ah ah ah ah ah   Ah ah ah ah ah ah ah.
Eh eh eh eh eh eh eh   Eh eh eh eh eh eh eh.
Ee ee ee ee ee ee ee   Ee ee ee ee ee ee ee.
Oh oh oh oh oh oh oh   Oh oh oh oh oh oh oh.
Oo oo oo oo oo oo oo   Oo oo oo oo oo oo oo.

This exercise also uses arpeggios, but this time you will hold for a moment at the top and descend singing each note of the major scale. Work with the open vowel Ah until you feel comfortable enough to expand to other vowels. You can also experiment with different tempos, slowing or speeding up the exercise.

Amazing Grace

  ## Amazing Grace Instrumental

Traditional Hymn
Arr. Michaela Anne Neller

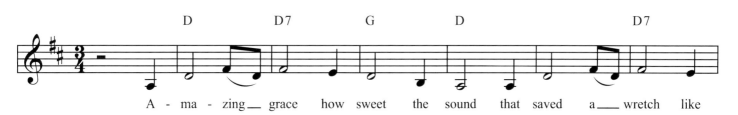

A - ma - zing grace how sweet the sound that saved a wretch like

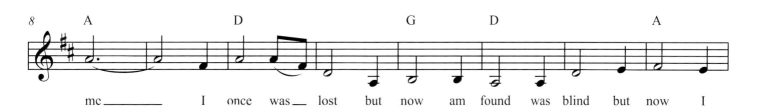

me I once was lost but now am found was blind but now I

see T'was Grace that taught my heart to fear And Grace my fears re -

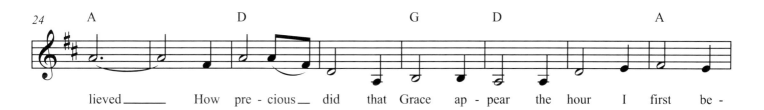

lieved How pre - cious did that Grace ap - pear the hour I first be -

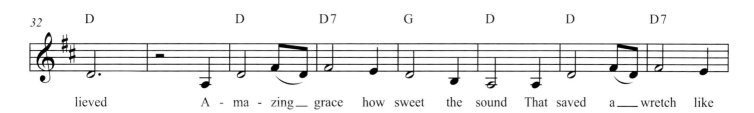

lieved A - ma - zing grace how sweet the sound That saved a wretch like

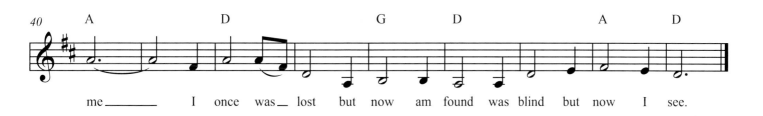

me I once was lost but now am found was blind but now I see.

29

Wildwood Flower

Wildwood Flower Instrumental

Traditional
Arr. Michaela Anne Neller

Oh I'll twine with my min - gles and wa - ving black hair
Oh I'll dance I will sing and my laugh shall be gay
Oh he taught me to love him and pro - mised to love
Oh he taught me to love him and called me his flow'r

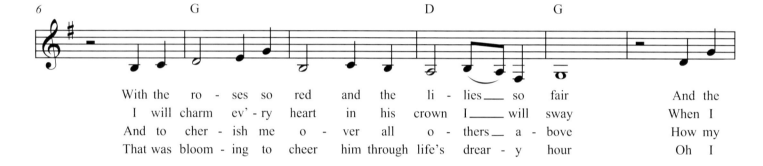

With the ro - ses so red and the li - lies so fair And the
I will charm ev' - ry heart in his crown I will sway When I
And to cher - ish me o - ver all o - thers a - bove How my
That was bloom - ing to cheer him through life's drear - y hour Oh I

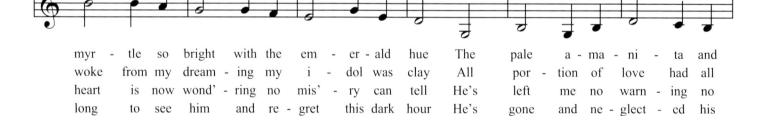

myr - tle so bright with the em - er - ald hue The pale a - ma - ni - ta and
woke from my dream - ing my i - dol was clay All por - tion of love had all
heart is now wond' - ring no mis' - ry can tell He's left me no warn - ing no
long to see him and re - gret this dark hour He's gone and ne - glect - ed his

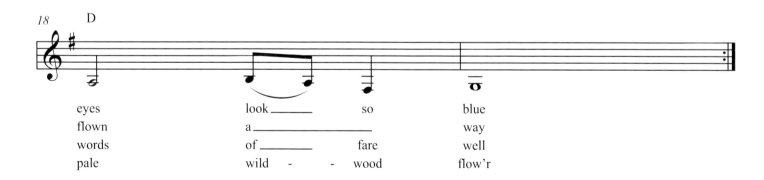

eyes look so blue
flown a way
words of fare well
pale wild - - wood flow'r

30

Gold Watch and Chain

  ## Gold Watch and Chain Instrumental

Traditional
Arr. Michaela Anne Neller

I will pawn you my gold watch and chain love. And I'll pawn you my gold wed-ding ring. I will pawn you this heart in my bos-om. On-ly say that you'll love me a-gain.

Dar-ling how could I stay here with out you. / Take back all these gifts you have giv-en.

I have no thing to ease my poor heart. This old world would seem sad love with out you. / Dia-mond ring and a lock of your hair. And a card with your pic-ture up on it.

Tell me now that we ne-ver will part. / It's a face that is false but is fair.

I will pawn you my gold watch and chain love. And I'll pawn you my gold wed-ding ring. I will pawn you this heart in my bos-om. On-ly say that you'll love me a-gain.

Angel Band

  ## Angel Band Instrumental

Traditional
Arr. Michaela Anne Neller

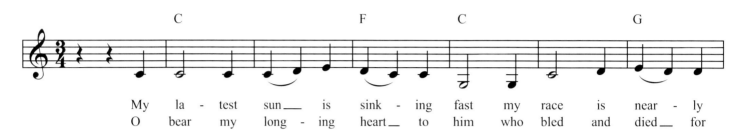

My la - test sun __ is sink - ing fast my race is near - ly
O bear my long - ing heart __ to him who bled and died __ for

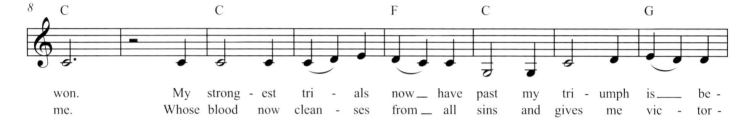

won. My strong - est tri - als now __ have past my tri - umph is __ be -
me. Whose blood now clean - ses from __ all sins and gives me vic - tor -

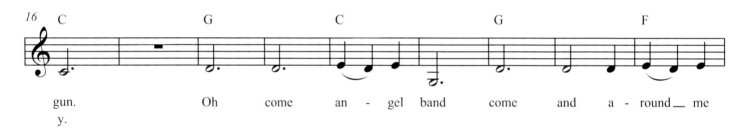

gun. Oh come an - gel band come and a - round __ me
y.

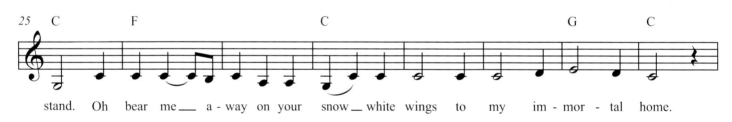

stand. Oh bear me __ a - way on your snow __ white wings to my im - mor - tal home.

Oh bear me __ a - way on your snow __ white wings to my im - mor - tal home.

Wayfaring Stranger

  ## Wayfaring Stranger Instrumental

Traditional
Arr. Michaela Anne Neller

Ease My Mind

  ## Ease My Mind Instrumental

Michaela Anne Neller

I've __ been go - ing in my round __ a - bout way. Show - ing
I've __ been ri - ding on this train __ it's too fast. But I got

you that I will love __ you al - ways. Know - ing that I'm gon - na
some where to be and __ it won't last. Sor - ry love there is no

need __ you some - day. But __ I got - ta be the one __ to say when
room __ in vis - ions. Sor - ry love I want to be __ the one left

I know that all the pat - ience in you _____ is used
I know that all the pat - ience in you _____ is used

lov - in' me __ Cause
lov - in' me __ Cause

I fear __ I fear that I won't be the one they love
I fear __ I fear that I won't do the things I love

And I fear __ I fear that I won't be here long e -
And I fear __ I fear that I won't be here long e -

nough.   And   I   fear _____   I   fear   a   life   of   fear   I

nough.   And   I   fear _____   I   fear   a   life   of   fear   I

know   it's   tough   so   take   my __   wor - ries and bring them

know   it's   tough   so   take   my __   wor - ries and bring them

to _____   the   sea   wash them __ with me

to _____   the   sea   wash them __ with me

ease   my __   mind _____   for   me.

ease   my __   mind _____   for   me.

Travelin' With You

  ## Travelin' With You Instrumental

Michaela Anne Neller

I've been think - ing I should leave ___ late - ly ___
Show I see ___ is less than what it could be ___

know-ing well ___ all that I'll be mis - sing ___ with you ___ you're
On - ly cause ___ I'm view-ing through the eyes ___ you gave me you're

ta - king ___ me ___ for ___ the ride of my life I can't ___ be trave -
ja - ding ___ my ___ view ___ til I can't be seen I can't ___ be trave -

lin' with you ___ ev' - ry time ___ I go to leave you take me ___
lin' with you ___ more and more ___ I want to go my own way ___

show-ing me ___ a world I would - n't see with - out you ___
take a risk ___ and feel the sun a - lone on ___ my back ___

I'd ra - ther ___ go out dis - co - ver a new I can't ___ be trave - lin' with you ___
out in ___ the ___ world ___ not hid - den from view I can't ___ be trave - lin' with you ___

36

Willow Tree

  ## Willow Tree Instrumental

Michaela Anne Neller

I've been wai - ting__ pa-tient - ly by__ that wil-low tree__ it__ weeps for me__

Ev - er since you__ went a - way you__ pro-mised you'd__ be__

back for me__ days go by__ and__ the clocks tick-ing__ and__ the

more I see__ how long I'll be__ wai - ting

Fly - ing through__ these clouds__ and__ rays I'm__ doubt-ing now that

I can stay__ the sta - ble stea - dy__ girl you see__ who

fo - llows through and__ will re - main__ here for you__ and__

38